To Isabella, Nicholas, and Michael

Always stay true to yourself and find your strengths in life. I am so proud of each of you every single day. Remember to surround yourself with people who make you happy, and continuously do the right thing even when no one is looking. You are all amazing-just the way you are!

Fidgety Frank Goes to Field Day

is meant to educate children on the value of inclusion and acceptance of students who have Attention Deficit Hyperactivity Disorder. ADHD is one of the most common neurodevelopmental disorders of childhood. Children with ADHD may have trouble paying attention, controlling impulsive behaviors, or simply be overly active. They may be unable to sit still, constantly fidget, daydream, and act without thinking. The story shows Fidgety Frank's struggles in the classroom and strengths outside on Field Day.

Fidgety Frank is ten years old and in the fourth grade. Today is the best day for Frank because today is FIELD DAY!

Frank loves Field Day. He loves to be outside running around and playing sports. However, today is tough for Frank because he has to wait all day in school for Field Day to begin. He already knows he will be daydreaming about it all day long.

"First things first," Ms. Wilson says to get her class ready for reading groups.

Frank looks for his books, but oh, what a mess his desk is! Books, pencils, fidgets, crayons, and shredded-up papers are scattered and piled up all over his work space.

Riley, who is always mean to Frank, asks, "Why is your desk always a mess?"

"I don't know," Frank replies. It makes him feel sad because she is not nice to him.

Sophia comforts her friend. "It's okay, Frank. I will help you get organized."

Sophia helps Frank put his books and pencils away. Frank and Sophia work together, and before long Frank's desk is clean and organized. Even though Frank is shy and has difficulty making friends, he tells Sophia, "Thank you."

Frank selects the correct book for his reading group. Sometimes Frank is embarrassed because reading is hard. Frank pushes his eraser around on his desk to see if he can wear it down during reading group. It makes a mess, and eraser shavings are everywhere!

The bell rings. It is time for lunch then recess. Frank is so relieved that he gets to leave his classroom.

Frank sits down in the cafeteria with his friends. Frank loves to play Flip The Bottle. Frank grabs his water bottle and flips it, and then this happens...

Water goes everywhere! He is soaked! His friends are soaked! The rest of the class is laughing and pointing at Frank and his big mess.

Riley rolls her eyes at him, "Oh my goodness, what did you do now?"

Sophia gives him some paper towels and tells the other kids to stop laughing.

Frank's last class before Field Day is art. The art teacher, Ms. Gomez instructs the students to draw a self-portrait. Frank is excited to do this. But as soon as Ms. Gomez starts giving the class directions, Frank starts daydreaming.

Ms. Gomez calls on Frank. He does not respond.

She says a little louder, "Frank."

Frank stares out the window daydreaming about Field Day.

This time the teacher calls even louder, "FRANK!"

The teacher asks him, "Did you hear what I said?"
Frank replies, "No."

Frank is distracted by the sounds of music coming from the room next door. Before Frank can finish his self-portrait, his teacher announces that class is over. The other kids complete their pictures, but Frank does not finish in time. Ms. Gomez tells Frank he can finish his drawing tomorrow.

Frank sighs and thinks to himself, "Ohhh no, another project I didn't finish."

He is bummed.

Here comes the announcement from the principal over the loudspeaker that Frank has been waiting for. "Students, the time has arrived! Field Day starts in five minutes. Pack up your belongings, and get your water bottles ready." Frank jumps up and runs to the door. "Frank!" yells his teacher, "You have to wait until I call your table."

Frank's head drops in disappointment as he heads back to his chair. The teacher begins calling tables, "Tables 1 and 2, please line up."

Frank waits patiently.
Frank tries so hard not to fidget in his seat, but he cannot control himself. The teacher continues until she finally calls for Table 5 to line up.

Frank jumps up to run toward the door. Lucky for him, Sophia reminds him to grab his water bottle. Frank grabs his water bottle and runs to the line. He is ready to go.

All of the classes head out to the field. Frank is happy because he can finally run around and get some energy out.

The teachers assign each class a team color. Frank's class is Blue, his favorite color. The Gym teacher makes announcements about all of the Field Day rules.

"Be kind, be respectful, and most of all, have fun!" she explains.

The first competition is the relay race. Frank is ready! He is determined to win first place. His team is up, and he is picked to be the final runner.

"On your mark... Get set... GO!" announces the Gym teacher.

Frank's team is off to a slow start, and they are quickly in last place. Frank is nervous, but he is so excited to run.

The Blue Team is behind the rest of the group and destined to finish last. Frank's heart pounds as Riley approaches him to hand off the baton. They make the handoff, and Frank runs fast!

Frank runs so fast that he is soon close to the other teams. He passes the Red Team, then the Pink Team. He passes the Yellow Team to take second place...

He is now head-to-head with the Green Team runner for first place. Everyone is screaming for Frank!

He did it! Frank finished first place! His whole team runs over to him in excitement to celebrate. Frank is so happy and so proud of himself.

Riley even says, "Wow, Frank, you sure are fast!"

The next event is the spoon race. The students have to balance an egg on a spoon from one end of the field to the other without dropping the egg. Frank is nervous about this one too, but he is confident he can do it. It is his turn, and he makes it end-to-end without dropping the egg.

Frank wins again!!! His teammates surround him and shout, "Frank! Frank! Frank!"

The final game to win first place is an obstacle course. Each student has to do jumping jacks, hop on one foot, complete sit-ups and pushups, then race to the finish line. The entire team has to make it across to the finish line to win first place. Each class gets to choose three students to represent them and compete for the gold medal.

Sophia says, "Frank, Sal, and Riley should compete for our team." Frank is so happy that Sophia and his teammates choose him.

Frank notices that Riley and Sal are both nervous. He tells them,

"Just try your best. Push yourself. Run as fast as you can. You got this!" Riley realizes how friendly and helpful Frank is, and she begins to feel bad for not being nice to Frank all the time.

All of the teams cheer as their teammates line up.

The announcer says, "Ready... Set... GO!"

The jumping jacks are first, followed by hopping on one foot. Riley is already out of breath and having a hard time finishing. Frank roots her on, saying, "Come on, Riley, you can do it!"

Frank keeps encouraging his team. "Don't give up," he yells The Red Team runs across the finish line first. Frank, Riley, and Sal finish in second place.

Next are the sit-ups and pushups. Frank is the first to finish, but he has to wait for the others because they must finish as a team. Riley is tired and about to quit. She begins to cry because she just cannot do all of her pushups.

Frank looks at her and says, "You got this! I believe in you."

Sal complains, "Come on, let's go! We're going to lose because of Riley."

Frank tells him, "No, we are not leaving her. We are a team."

Riley finally finishes. Frank shouts, "Let's go. We can still win!"

The three teammates run as fast as they can to the finish line, but the Red Team wins first place.

Riley is so sad and upset. She blames herself for her team's loss.

Frank tells her, "We win as a team, and we lose as a team."

His support makes her feel better. She grabs Frank, hugs him, and apologizes for being mean to him before.

Frank feels confident and happy about the day. He smiles and walks back into school with all of his friends.

About the Author

Dr. Jennifer L. Nangano has been a School Psychologist since December 2015. Prior to working in the public school system, she worked as a Director at a Center for Adults with Disabilities and as a Supervisor for 10 years on a crisis team for a Regional Medical Center.

Dr. Nangano received her B.A. in Psychology from Seton Hall University in 2002 and went on to receive an M.A. in Psychological Counseling from Monmouth University in 2004. In 2012, she received a Doctorate Degree from Walden University in Psychology, with a specialization in School Psychology. Dr. Nangano has spoken at several conferences and workshops throughout the state of New Jersey. She is the author of "Psychiatric Inpatient Treatment, Intellectual Disability, and Mental Illness in a Dual Diagnosis Psychiatric Unit." Dr. Nangano enjoys spending time with her family and advocating for children and adults with special needs.

www.ingramcontent.com/pod-product-compliance
Lightning Source LLC
LaVergne TN
LVHW072115060526
838201LV00011B/244